3DAY
WHOLE FOOD
PRESSURE COOKER CHALLENGE

Quick, Easy and Delicious **Whole Food Electric Pressure Cooker Recipes** for Vibrant Health and Weight Loss

Published by The Fruitful Mind
www.fruitfulbooks.com

Disclaimer

Introduction

No matter who you are, you probably have an opinion on nutrition. It's a highly-contested topic, with a seemingly never-ending list of "recommendations." Go vegan, people tell you. Only eat "low carb." There are even some people out there who insist that eating only fruit is a viable way to stay alive—and get trim.

But what if the single thing you need to do to stay slim, fight diseases, and feel like "yourself" again (before you had to worry about what you put in your mouth) was simply this:

Focus on whole foods.

It sounds simple, but it's not. How often have you reached for processed foods, things that are frozen or canned, just to throw something together in the kitchen? If you're like most North Americans (and the rest of the world, increasingly), you've done that frequently, widening your waistlines in the process.

But eating whole foods—the kinds that are usually found on the outer aisles of the grocery store, and not in the inner aisles (that's where the processed junk is hidden, think meat counter, fish counter, fruits, and vegetables)—helps you dive back to the ways in which your eternally-slim grandmother ate. She stuck with vegetables, meats, fish, fruit: things with nutrition, which stuck to your bones. Foods that help you keep moving, day after day, and with enough spices to make it taste delicious.

This book uses the electric pressure cooker, or the famous time-saving "Pressure Cooker" to create nutritional, slimming, whole food-based recipes. It asks you to do 30 days of whole foods, and whole foods only. And because your body is able to create new habits after just 21 days, 30 days allows you to stick to those habits. It breeds a path toward commitment. And it refuses to let you fail.

With the whole food diet, you can look forward to looking younger, having stronger teeth and bones, decreasing your risk for heart disease and certain cancers, and decreasing your risk of diabetes.

And beyond that, whole foods mean no commitment to "brands." You aren't paying a single penny toward advertising. That means you'll probably save money on the way—something you thought you were doing when tossing together processed foods.

Good luck on this journey toward better health. You deserve it, and now, you're finally giving yourself the time to try.

TABLE OF CONTENTS

WHOLE FOOD
BREAKFAST PRESSURE COOKER RECIPES

Hard Boiled Eggs in the Pressure Cooker

SERVES
6

MINUTES
10

Nutritional Information Per Egg: 63 calories, .3 grams carbohydrates, 5.5 grams protein, 4.4 grams fat, 62 mg sodium, 1.4 grams saturated fat.

Ingredients:

1 cup water

6 eggs (pasture-raised is preferable)

Directions:

First, add one cup of the water to your Pressure Cooker.

Add a steamer basket or a stainless steel strainer to the Pressure Cooker. Place the eggs in the steamer basket, and then place the lid on the Pressure Cooker.

Turn on the Pressure Cooker, and press the button that says "MANUAL."

Next, using the plus and minus buttons, adjust the amount of time to eight minutes.

Place the lid on the Pressure Cooker and seal it, ensuring that the vent is closed. Next, allow the Pressure Cooker to cook for the desired eight minutes. After eight minutes, do a manual release of the pressure—releasing the valve. Allow the Pressure Cooker to cool for about two minutes. Then, remove the lid carefully, ensuring that the steam escapes away from your face.

Remove the eggs from the Pressure Cooker and allow them to cool prior to enjoying.

Tiny Omelets for Quick Grab-and-Go Meals

SERVES
6

MINUTES
15

Nutritional Information Per Serving: 86 calories, 1.9 grams carbohydrates, 8.3 grams protein, 5 grams fat, 52 mg sodium, 2.3 grams saturated fat.

Ingredients:

4 eggs

2 tbsp. almond milk

1/2 cup ground beef

1/2 diced onion

1/4 diced green pepper

1/2 tsp. onion powder

1/2 tsp. garlic powder

With 6 silicone baking cups

Directions:

First, whisk together the eggs, almond milk, ground beef, onion, green pepper, onion powder, and garlic powder in a mixing bowl. When it's well-assimilated, simply pour the omelet mixture into your six silicone baking cups at the bottom of the Pressure Cooker (in the steamer).

Next, place the lid on the Pressure Cooker and set the Pressure Cooker to MANUAL. Use the plus and minus buttons to set the Pressure Cooker to 12 minutes.

After 10 minutes of cooking, release the pressure manually—making sure that the steam escapes away from your face.

Allow the mini omelets to cool for about two minutes prior to removing and either serving or refrigerating for later use.

Squash and Apple Porridge

SERVES
3

MINUTES
20

Nutritional Information Per Serving: 112 calories, 23 grams carbohydrates, 6 grams protein, 0.5 grams fat, 434 mg sodium, 0 grams saturated fat.

Ingredients:

2 very large apples

1 squash

1 tsp. cinnamon

3/4 cup bone broth

1/4 tsp. ginger

1/4 tsp. cloves

1/2 tsp. salt

Directions:

First, add the squash, without cutting it, to the Pressure Cooker. Add the apple around it, in chunks. Net, add the spices and the bone broth. Place the lid on the Pressure Cooker, and secure it. Close the steam valve, and press the button that says "Manual." Cook the squash mixture for eight minutes.

Next, when the timer beeps, allow the pressure to release naturally for eight minutes. Afterwards, press the button that says "CANCEL," and remove the lid, making sure to release the pressure away from your face. Remove the Pressure Cooker's lid, and allow the interior to cool.

After it's cooled for about three or four minutes, place the squash on the cutting board and slice it in half, long-ways. Remove the interior seeds. Then, place both sides of the squash, apples, broth, and spices (from the inside of the Pressure Cooker) in a blender.

Blend the mixture for about 30 seconds. It should be smooth. Serve the mixture warm, cold, or however you like, and enjoy.

Meaty Quiche Sans the Crust

SERVES
4

MINUTES
40

Nutritional Information Per Serving: 255 calories, 2.9 grams carbohydrates, 20 grams fat, 16 grams protein, 606 mg sodium, 10.2 grams saturated fat.

Ingredients:

6 eggs

1/2 cup almond milk

1 cup ground sausage, already cooked

1/2 tsp. sea salt

1/2 tsp. black pepper

4 slices turkey bacon, already cooked and crumbled

2 sliced green onions

1 cup water

Directions:

First, place the Pressure Cooker's metal trivet at the bottom. Add a cup of water to the Pressure Cooker at this time.

Next, whisk together the almond milk, salt, pepper, and the eggs in a side mixing bowl.

Next, add the sausage, bacon, and the green onions to a quick dish (I used a soufflé dish, but any baking dish will probably do, as long as it fits into your Pressure Cooker).

Pour the egg mixture over the top of the sausage mixture. Stir to combine the two mixtures.

Next, add aluminum foil over the top of the quiche dish, putting it on loosely. Create a "sling" of aluminum foil to put beneath the baking dish, so that you can yank it out afterwards without burning yourself.

Place the baking dish in the Pressure Cooker, and place the lid on the top. Lock it, and put the Pressure Cooker on HIGH pressure for 30 minutes.

After the Pressure Cooker beeps, allow the pot to release pressure naturally for 10 minutes. After 10 minutes, use the "quick pressure" method to release the pressure quickly, making sure to avoid any steam contact with your face.

Remove the lid very carefully and remove the quiche dish from the Pressure Cooker using the aluminum foil sling. Remove the aluminum foil on the top and serve the quiche warm.

WHOLE FOOD

SOUPS & SALADS PRESSURE COOKER RECIPES

Chowder with Buffalo Chicken

SERVES
6

MINUTES
18

Nutritional Information Per Serving: 384 calories, 17 grams carbohydrates, 39 grams protein, 16 grams fat, 875 mg sodium, 10.2 grams saturated fat.

Ingredients:

1 tbsp. olive oil

1 1/2 pounds chicken

1 cup diced carrots

1 1/4 cups diced celery

1 diced onion

1 1/2 cups diced sweet potatoes

6 cups chicken broth

1 cup Frank's hot sauce (definitely compliant, made of whole foods)

1 cup coconut milk, full-fat

1/3 cup chopped cilantro

Directions:

First, press the "sauté" button on the Pressure Cooker. Add the olive oil to the bottom of the Pressure Cooker, and then sauté the onion in the oil for three minutes. Press the CANCEL button at this time.

Next, add the sweet potatoes, celery, carrots, and the chicken to the Pressure Cooker. Add the chicken broth over the top, along with the Frank's hot sauce. Stir well.

Place the lid on the Pressure Cooker and seal it into place.

Press the MANUAL button and cook the chicken soup on HIGH pressure for a full 13 minutes. After 13 minutes, use the quick release method, making sure to release the steam away from your face. Remove the lid at this time.

Next, shred the chicken using two forks. Add the coconut milk to the soup, and stir well. Serve with the cilantro, and enjoy.

Chicken Soup with Zucchini Noodles

SERVES
8

MINUTES
15

Nutritional Information Per Serving: 184 calories, 6.3 grams carbohydrates, 3.8 grams fat, 29 grams protein, 645 mg sodium, 1.1 grams saturated fat.

Ingredients:

1 1/2 pounds chicken

1 1/4 cup chopped carrots

1 diced onion

6 cups chicken broth

1/3 cup apple cider vinegar

1 bay leaf

1 tbsp. chopped rosemary, fresh

1 tbsp. chopped thyme, fresh

1 tsp. dried dill

2 tsp. lemon pepper

2 zucchinis, spiralized

Directions:

First, place the chicken, carrots, onion, chicken broth, apple cider vinegar, bay leaf, rosemary, thyme, dill, and lemon pepper in the Pressure Cooker. Give the mixture a good stir.

Next, place the lid on the Pressure Cooker, and cook on HIGH pressure for 11 minutes.

After 11 minutes, use the quick release option to release the steam immediately. Make sure you release the steam away from your face. Remove the lid at this time, and shred the chicken using two forks. Then, add the zucchini noodles to the mixture, along with any salt and pepper.

Serve warm, and enjoy.

Sweetie Potato Chunky Soup

SERVES
6

MINUTES
20

Nutritional Information Per Serving: 342 calories, 39 grams carbohydrates, 20 grams fat, 4.5 grams protein, 675 mg sodium, 16 grams saturated fat.

Ingredients:

2 sweet potatoes, diced and peeled

1/2 diced onion

1 tbsp. coconut oil

1 diced red pepper

1 diced zucchini

2 1/2-inch piece of ginger, chopped roughly

3 minced garlic cloves

14 ounces coconut milk

1 tsp. salt

1 tsp. pepper

2 tbsp. Thai red curry paste

2 tsp. curry powder

14 ounces tomatoes, diced

Juice from 2 limes

1/2 cup chopped cilantro, or more to taste

Directions:

First, press the button that says "sauté" on the Pressure Cooker. Once the pot grows hot, add the coconut oil and the onion. Sauté the onion for four minutes. Then, add the ginger, along with the garlic. Cook for an additional three minutes, stirring occasionally.

Next, add the tomatoes and the rest of the vegetables, including the sweet potatoes. Stir well, and add the salt, the spices, and the Thai curry paste. Stir well.

Next, add the coconut milk slowly, stirring gradually to ensure everything is well-mixed. When it is, press the button that says "cancel" on the Pressure Cooker.

Place the lid on the Pressure Cooker at this time. Secure it into place, and press the MANUAL button.

Cook on HIGH pressure for five minutes. After five minutes, release the pressure immediately— allowing the steam to escape.

Afterwards, remove the lid and add the juice from two limes. Stir well. Garnish the soup with the chopped cilantro, and serve warm.

South of the Border Soup

SERVES
6

MINUTES
20

Nutritional Information Per Serving: 505 calories, 34 grams carbohydrates, 46 grams protein, 22 grams fat, 943 mg sodium, 13 grams saturated fat.

Ingredients:

2 tbsp. coconut oil

4 diced red peppers

1 3/4 pound ground beef

1 diced onion

2 tbsp. cumin

3 tbsp. chili powder

1 tsp. paprika

2 tsp. salt

1/2 tsp. garlic powder

1 tsp. cinnamon

25 ounces tomatoes, diced

20 ounces bone broth

1/2 tsp. onion powder

1/8 tsp cayenne pepper

6 ounces green chilies, diced

6 ounces coconut milk

Directions:

First, turn on the Pressure Cooker and press the button that says "sauté." Next, add the coconut oil to the Pressure Cooker, allowing it to melt.

When the coconut oil melts, add the peppers and the onion, and sauté for eight minutes, stirring occasionally.

Next, add the ground beef to the Pressure Cooker. Stir well and cook until the beef isn't pink any longer. Drain the beef at this time through a colander to get out the excess juice, and then add the beef back to the Pressure Cooker.

Next, add the rest of the spices, and stir. Then, add the tomatoes, coconut milk, and the broth. Stir well, and then add the green chilies.

Next, place the lid on the Pressure Cooker, and seal it. Press the button that says "Soup," and then press the "minus" button so that the pot reads back the cooking time of 25 minutes.

Allow the Pressure Cooker to pressure cook now. When it beeps, release the pressure immediately, making sure that the steam is released away from your face. Remove the lid at this time, and give the mixture a good stir before serving.

Gingered Carrot Soup

SERVES
6

MINUTES
35

Nutritional Information Per Serving: 234 calories, 17 grams carbohydrates, 3 grams protein, 18 grams fat, 296 mg sodium, 16 grams saturated fat.

Ingredients:

1 diced onion

1 tbsp. coconut oil

4 tbsp. chopped ginger, fresh

1 1/4 pounds carrots, chopped and peeled

6 cups vegetable stock

14 ounces coconut milk

1/2 tsp. salt

1/2 tsp. pepper

Directions:

First, turn on the Pressure Cooker, and press the button that says "sauté." When it heats up, add the coconut oil to the Pressure Cooker, and then add the onions. Allow the onions to sauté for four minutes. Then, add the ginger and the garlic. Sauté for an additional three minutes.

Next, CANCEL the Pressure Cooker's sauté function, and add the broth and the carrots. Place the lid on the Pressure Cooker at this time, and secure it into place.

Press the "Manual" function on the Pressure Cooker, and cook on HIGH pressure for seven minutes.

After seven minutes, release the pressure manually. Add the coconut milk and any salt and pepper to taste, and stir well.

Next, use either an immersion blender or a regular blender (which will require you to blend in batches) to blend the soup to your desired consistency. Serve the soup warm, and enjoy.

Sweet Potato Curry

SERVES
6

MINUTES
40

Nutritional Information Per Serving: 381 calories, 25 grams carbohydrates, 26 grams protein, 20 grams fat, 194 mg sodium, 16 mg saturated fat.

Ingredients:

1/2 diced onion

2 tsp. coconut oil

1 pound chicken, diced into bite-sized pieces

4 minced garlic cloves

1 cup chicken broth

2 cups diced sweet potatoes

2 cups diced green beans

1 diced red pepper

3 tbsp. curry powder

1/2 tsp. cayenne pepper

1 tsp. turmeric

14 ounces coconut milk

Directions:

First, press the "sauté" button on the Pressure Cooker. Add the coconut oil, garlic, and the onion to the Pressure Cooker, and sauté for four minutes.

At this time, press the "Manual" button, and set the pressure to HIGH.

Add the sweet potatoes, chicken, green beans, red pepper, chicken broth, and the spices, and stir well.

Place the lid on the Pressure Cooker, and cook the curry on HIGH pressure for 12 minutes.

After 12 minutes, release the pressure immediately, taking the valve from "seal" to "vent." Next, after the pressure is completely released, remove the lid and press the "sauté" button once more.

Add the coconut milk to the mixture, and allow it to heat for three minutes. Stir slowly, every minute or so. Your curry is ready to eat.

Butternut Squash Soup

SERVES
6

MINUTES
30

Nutritional Information Per Serving: 242 calories, 35 grams carbohydrates, 6 grams protein, 10 grams fat, 787 mg sodium, 5.3 grams saturated fat.

Ingredients:

1 butternut squash

2 tbsp. olive oil

2 pounds pumpkin (one generally used for pie)

1 apple

3 minced garlic cloves

1 diced onion

3 cups vegetable broth

2 tsp. basil, dried

2 tsp. sage, dried

2 tbsp. apple cider vinegar

1 tsp. salt

1/2 cup coconut milk

Directions:

First, peel the skin off of the butternut squash and sliced it in half, length-wise. Then, remove the seeds, and slice the squash into bite-sized pieces.

To prep the pumpkin, simply slice it into two pieces and take out the seeds. Slice the pumpkin into bite-sized pieces, just as you did with the squash. You can eat the skin if you wish.

Next, press the button that says "sauté" on the Pressure Cooker. Pour the olive oil into the Pressure Cooker, and then cook the onion for three minutes. Afterwards, add the garlic, and cook for an additional three minutes.

Next, after slicing the apple, add the pumpkin, squash, and the apple to the Pressure Cooker. Stir, and then add the apple cider vinegar, the spices, and the broth. Stir well, and place the lid on the Pressure Cooker at this time.

Next, select the "Manual" button, and cook on HIGH pressure for 14 minutes. Afterwards, allow the pressure to release naturally for 15 minutes. Then, release the rest of the pressure.

At this time, add the coconut milk, along with salt and pepper to taste. Use an immersion blender to blend the soup to your desired consistency. Serve the pumpkin soup warm, and enjoy.

Lettuce Wraps with Beef

SERVES
8

MINUTES
40

Nutritional Information Per Serving: 340 calories, 8.7 grams carbohydrates, 35 grams protein, 17 grams fat, 761 mg sodium, 8.4 grams saturated fat.

Ingredients:

2 cup onion, diced

2 tbsp. olive oil

1 tbsp. minced garlic

Juice from 1 lime

2 tbsp. minced ginger

2 pounds of beef, sliced

1/2 cup Thai curry paste, red

2 tbsp. ghee

1/2 cup water

3/4 cup diced tomatoes, from a can is fine

1/2 cup coconut milk

1 tsp. salt

1 tsp. pepper

3 tbsp. arrowroot powder mixed with 3 tbsp. of water, for thickening

Head of lettuce, for the wraps

Toppings for the wraps: avocado, purple cabbage, cilantro, and shredded carrots

Directions:

First, press the button on the Pressure Cooker that says "sauté." Then, when the Pressure Cooker is hot enough, pour the olive oil into the bottom, along with the onion. Allow the onion to cook for three minutes.

At this time, add the sliced beef. Cook the beef for about four minutes, or until it begins to brown.

Next, add the ginger, garlic, juice from the lime, curry paste, tomatoes, water, and the ghee. Stir well, and place the lid on the Pressure Cooker. Secure it.

Next, press the "Cancel" button on the Pressure Cooker. Put the Pressure Cooker on "Manual," and cook on HIGH pressure for a full 12 minutes. Afterwards, allow the pressure to release naturally.

Next, remove the lid from the Pressure Cooker. Add the arrowroot and water mixture, along with the coconut milk. Give the mixture a stir. Allow it to sit for five minutes, while you tear off lettuce pieces to create the "wraps."

Next, add toppings to the inside of the lettuce wraps: cilantro, shredded carrots, cabbage, and avocado, or whatever you like. Portion out the beef in the lettuce wraps, and serve.

Lighter Side Chicken Salad

SERVES
6

MINUTES
30

Nutritional Information Per Serving: 339 calories, 6.9 grams carbohydrates, 8 grams fat, 57 grams protein, 326 mg sodium, 2 grams saturated fat.

Ingredients:

2 1/2 pounds of chicken, sliced into bite-sized pieces

1 tbsp. olive oil or ghee

1 diced onion

1/2 tsp. salt

4 minced garlic cloves

1/2 pound mushrooms, sliced

1 1/2 cups cherry tomatoes

2 tbsp. tomato paste

1/2 tsp. black pepper, cracked

1/2 cup sliced green olives

1/2 cup chopped basil leaves

1/2 cup chopped Italian parsley

Directions:

First, salt the chicken pieces, and then press the "sauté" button on the Pressure Cooker.

Add the olive oil or ghee, and then add the mushrooms, onions, and a bit more salt, to taste. Stir well and allow the vegetables to soften. This should take about five minutes.

At this time, add the tomato paste and the garlic, and cook for about 45 seconds. The garlic should be fragrant.

Next, add the cherry tomatoes and the green olives to the mixture. Stir well, and add the chicken.

Next, add the lid to the top of the Pressure Cooker, and lock it into place. Press the "Manual" button and set the timer to eight minutes.

When the Pressure Cooker beeps, remove the lid immediately, making sure to release the steam away from your face. Add the black pepper, basil and parsley at this time, and give the mixture a stir.

Serve the light salad warm, and enjoy.

Chicken and Broccoli Salad

SERVES
2

MINUTES
20

Nutritional Information Per Serving: 465 calories, 10 grams carbohydrates, 71 grams protein, 14 grams fat, 1080 mg sodium, 3 grams saturated fat.

Ingredients:

1 pound of chicken, sliced into smaller strips

1 tsp. fish sauce

1/2 cup chicken broth

1 tbsp. Sesame oil

1/3 cup coconut aminos

1/2 tsp. sea salt

1/2 tsp. Pepper

1/2 tsp. red pepper flakes

10 ounces broccoli, chopped into pieces

1/2 tsp. apple cider vinegar

2 tbsp. water mixed with 2 tbsp. arrowroot powder

Directions:

First, add the sliced chicken to the Pressure Cooker. Pour over the fish sauce, chicken broth, sesame oil, coconut aminos, sea salt, pepper, and the red pepper flakes. Stir well, and place the lid on the Pressure Cooker.

Press the button that says "Manual," and set the timer for eight minutes. When the beeper sounds, release the pressure manually, making sure to release the steam away from your face.

To the side, stir together the water and the arrowroot powder. Once mixed, pour this mixture into the Pressure Cooker, stirring to combine.

Next, press the "sauté" button. Add the broccoli to the mixture at this time, and cook for five minutes, stirring every thirty seconds or so. The broccoli should be softer, and the sauce should be thick.

Pour the apple cider vinegar into the mixture at this time, and stir well. Serve the broccoli and chicken salad warm, and enjoy.

WHOLE FOOD
CHICKEN PRESSURE COOKER RECIPES

Chicken Cacciatore

SERVES
4

MINUTES
35

Nutritional Information Per Serving: 459 calories, 6 grams carbohydrates, 62 grams protein, 19 grams fat, 769 mg sodium, 4.8 grams saturated fat.

Ingredients:

4 chicken thighs, with the bone and without the skin

1 tbsp. olive oil

1 tsp. salt

1 tsp. pepper

14 ounces diced tomatoes

1/3 cup diced red pepper

1/3 cup diced onion

1/3 cup diced green pepper

1 tsp. oregano, dried

2 tbsp. chopped parsley

1 bay leaf

Directions:

First, salt and pepper the chicken.

Press the button that says "sauté" at this time, and add the olive oil. Add the chicken over the top of the olive oil, and brown the chicken on all sides for about three minutes. Then, set the chicken to the side.

Next, add the peppers and the onions to the Pressure Cooker. Sauté the mixture until they're soft, for about five minutes.

Then, pour the tomatoes into the Pressure Cooker, and add the chicken, bay leaf, oregano, and any extra salt and pepper to taste. Give the mixture a stir, and then place the lid on the Pressure Cooker at this time.

Cook the cacciatore on HIGH pressure for 25 minutes. Afterwards, allow the pressure to release naturally.

Afterwards, remove the lid, and toss out the bay leaf. Garnish the mixture with parsley, and serve warm.

Garlic Chicken with Lemon

SERVES
8

MINUTES
20

Nutritional Information Per Serving: 198 calories, 2.3 grams carbohydrates, 33 grams protein, 5.2 grams fat, 354 mg sodium, 2 grams saturated fat.

Ingredients:

2 pounds chicken

1 tbsp. ghee

1 tsp. sea salt

1 diced onion

1/2 tsp. paprika

1 tsp. dried parsley

6 minced garlic cloves

1/2 cup chicken broth

Juice from one lemon

3 tsp. Arrowroot flour, for thickening

Directions:

First, press the button on the Pressure Cooker that says "sauté." Then, add the ghee and the onion to the bottom of the Pressure Cooker, and sauté the onions for ten minutes. They should begin to brown.

At this time, add the chicken, salt, paprika, parsley, garlic, chicken broth, and the juice from your lemon to the Pressure Cooker, and give the mixture a stir.

Place the lid on the Pressure Cooker, and press the button that says "Poultry." Make sure the valve is closed. Allow the Pressure Cooker to cook on the poultry setting until it beeps.

After it beeps, release the pressure manually, making sure the steam escapes away from your face.

Next, take out about a 1/3 cup of the sauce inside the Pressure Cooker and add it to a mixing bowl. Add the arrowroot powder to this mixture, and stir. Then, pour this mixture into the Pressure Cooker once more. Stir.

Serve the chicken at this time, with the thickened sauce over the top.

Chicken Stroganoff

SERVES
6

MINUTES
25

Nutritional Information Per Serving: 305 calories, 3.7 grams carbohydrates, 41 grams protein, 13 grams fat, 573 mg sodium, 6.1 grams saturated fat.

Ingredients:

1 3/4 pounds chicken, sliced into pieces

2 tbsp. olive oil

10 ounces mushrooms, sliced

3/4 cup chicken broth

4 minced garlic cloves

2 tbsp. Arrowroot starch

1 tbsp. apple cider vinegar

2 tbsp. coconut aminos

1/2 cup coconut milk

1 tsp. salt

1 tsp. pepper

Directions:

First, press the button that says "sauté" on the Pressure Cooker. Add the olive oil to the bottom of the Pressure Cooker at this time.

To the side, toss together the arrowroot powder and the chicken in a ziplock bag or in a medium-sized mixing bowl. When the chicken is covered, add the chicken to the Pressure Cooker.

Sauté the chicken for around two minutes on each side, so that it begins to brown.

Next, add the mushrooms and the garlic to the mixture. After stirring for one minute, press the button that says "cancel."

Next, to the side, stir together the coconut aminos and the apple cider vinegar, along with the chicken broth. Pour this mixture over the chicken and the mushrooms.

At this time, add the lid to the Pressure Cooker, and secure the lid. Press the "Manual" function, and cook the mixture on HIGH for eight minutes.

Afterwards, allow the Pressure Cooker to release its pressure naturally. This should take about 15 minutes. After 15 minutes, release any leftover pressure, and remove the lid.

Pour the coconut milk into the Pressure Cooker at this time, and stir well. Press the "Cancel" button, and then press the "sauté" button once more. Allow the mixture to thicken for the next ten minutes on sauté, and then press the cancel button. Serve the chicken stroganoff warm, and enjoy.

Curried Chicken

SERVES
6

MINUTES
40

Nutritional Information Per Serving: 503 calories, 4.8 grams carbohydrates, 67 grams protein, 22 grams fat, 350 mg sodium, 16 grams saturated fat.

Ingredients:

14 ounces coconut milk, full fat

1 tsp. turmeric

1/3 cup lemon juice

1 tbsp. curry powder

3 pounds chicken

1/2 tsp. lemon zest

1/2 tsp. salt

Directions:

First, stir together the lemon juice, coconut milk, and all the spices in a side bowl. Pour a small bit of this into the Pressure Cooker, so that it coats the bottom.

Next, add the chicken to the Pressure Cooker. Add the rest of the coconut milk mixture over the top.

Place the lid on the Pressure Cooker and seal it into place. Press the "Poultry" button, and allow the Pressure Cooker to 'do its thing'. After the Pressure Cooker beeps, release the pressure manually, making sure that the steam escapes away from your face.

Next, use two forks to shred the chicken in the Pressure Cooker, and stir well. Add the lemon zest at this time, along with any salt to taste. Serve warm, and enjoy.

South of the Border Chicken

SERVES
4

MINUTES
20

Nutritional Information Per Serving: 473 calories, 8 grams carbohydrates, 61 grams protein, 21 grams fat, 11 grams saturated fat, 974 mg sodium.

Ingredients:

1 3/4 pounds chicken, sliced into pieces

1 tbsp. olive oil

1 tsp. garlic powder

1 tsp. paprika

1 tbsp. chili powder

1/2 tsp. cayenne pepper

1 sliced green pepper

1 sliced red pepper

1/3 cup lime juice

1 1/4 cup chicken broth

1 tbsp. water mixed with 1 tbsp. arrowroot starch

3/4 cup coconut milk, with the full fat

1/2 cup chopped cilantro for after cooking

1 tsp. salt

1 tsp. pepper (or to taste)

Directions:

First, press the "sauté" button on the Pressure
Cooker. This will "preheat" your pot.

To the side, stir together the garlic powder, paprika,
chili powder, and the cayenne pepper until well
mixed. Rub the mixture over the chicken, and keep
any spices that are leftover.

Next, pour olive oil into the bottom of the Pressure
Cooker, making sure to coat it. Add the chicken and
cook it for about two minutes on each side,
browning it. Press the "Cancel" button after you've
browned it on all sides.

Next, pour the lime juice, chicken broth, and the rest
of the ingredients into the Pressure Cooker, along
with the red and green peppers.

Place the lid on the Pressure Cooker at this time. Press the "Manual" button, and cook the chicken on HIGH for eight minutes.

Afterwards, release the pressure manually, making sure to keep the steam away from your face as you release.

Next, remove the lid, and add the coconut milk to the mixture. To the side, stir together the arrowroot and the water, and pour this mixture into the Pressure Cooker as well. Allow the mixture to sit for three minutes, thickening.

Now, stir the mixture, and add salt and pepper to taste. Serve the mixture warm, and enjoy.

Chicken Shawarma

SERVES
8

MINUTES
20

Nutritional Information Per Serving: 170 calories, .8 grams carbohydrates, 30 grams protein, 3.8 grams fat, 317 mg sodium, .1 grams saturated fat.

Ingredients:

2 1/2 pounds boneless chicken, either thighs or breasts or a combination of both

1/2 tsp. turmeric

1 tsp. cumin

1/2 tsp. garlic powder

1/4 tsp. allspice

1/2 tsp. cinnamon

1/2 tsp. chili powder

1/2 tsp. salt

1/2 tsp. pepper

1 cup chicken broth

Directions:

First, slice the chicken into strips. Place the strips in your Pressure Cooker.

To the side, stir together the spices: turmeric, cumin, garlic powder, allspice, cinnamon, chili powder, salt, and pepper. Pour the spices over the chicken, and use your hands to really grind the spices into the chicken.

Next, pour the chicken broth over the chicken, and place the lid on the Pressure Cooker. Press the "poultry" button, and change the timer to 15 minutes.

After the timer beeps, allow the Pressure Cooker to release pressure naturally for 10 minutes. After 10 minutes, release the pressure manually, making sure that you release it away from your face.

Serve the chicken warm, and enjoy.

WHOLE FOOD
FISH PRESSURE COOKER RECIPES

Pressure Cooker Salmon with Lemon Pepper

SERVES
4

MINUTES
15

Nutritional Information Per Serving: 239 calories, .2 grams carbohydrates, 22 grams protein, 17 grams fat, 343 mg sodium, 9.8 grams saturated fat.

Ingredients:

1 cup water

1 pound salmon, with the skin still on

2 sprigs basil

1 sprig parsley

1/2 sliced lemon

1/2 tsp. salt

1/2 tsp. pepper

3 tbsp. coconut oil

Directions:

First, place the water and the basil and parsley in the Pressure Cooker. Add the steamer rack above the water, with the handles upward. Next, place the salmon on the steamer, with the skin down.

Next, melt the coconut oil either on the stovetop or in the microwave, and drizzle the mixture over the salmon. Season the salmon with both pepper and salt, and then cover the salmon with the slices of the lemon.

Next, place the lid on the Pressure Cooker, and turn the vent to the "sealing" function. Plug in the Pressure Cooker, and press the "steam" button. Press the plus and minus buttons to set the Pressure Cooker to just 3 minutes.

When the Pressure Cooker beeps, release the pressure inside the Pressure Cooker quickly, making sure that you keep the steam away from your face. At this time, press the "cancel" button, and remove the lid.

Immediately, remove the steamer rack, with the salmon on it, using gloves so that you don't burn your hands.

Slice and serve the salmon warm, and enjoy.

Gumbo with Shrimp and Sausage

SERVES
4

MINUTES
30

Nutritional Information Per Serving: 552 calories, 12 grams carbohydrates, 55 grams protein, 30 grams fat, 1517 mg sodium, 13 grams saturated fat.

Ingredients:

10 ounces turkey sausage, sliced into pieces

2 tbsp. coconut oil

2 celery stalks, diced

1 diced red pepper

14 ounces diced tomatoes

1 diced onion

1 cup chicken broth

1 pound of shrimp, either peeled or unpeeled

2 tbsp. Cajun seasoning

2 bay leaves

1/2 tsp. salt

1/2 tsp. pepper

3 tbsp. chopped parsley

Directions:

First, add the coconut oil to the Pressure Cooker, and press the button that says "sauté." When the coconut oil melts, add the sliced sausage, and allow it to brown for about three minutes on each side. When it has, remove it to a side plate.

Next, add the onion, pepper, celery, and the Cajun seasoning to the Pressure Cooker and cook for three minutes, stirring occasionally. Press the button that says "Cancel" at this time.

Next, add the tomatoes, stock, bay leaves, and the sausage to the Pressure Cooker, and give the mixture a good stir.

Place the lid on the Pressure Cooker at this time, and set the Pressure Cooker to "sealing." Press the "Manual" button, making sure the time reads back "5 minutes."

When the Pressure Cooker beeps, press the "Cancel" button. Release the pressure manually, making sure the steam escapes away from your face.

At this time, remove the lid, and press the "sauté" button." Add the shrimp at this time, and cook for four minutes on "sauté," or until the shrimp are no longer see-through.

Next, add salt and pepper to taste. Serve the mixture with the parsley over the top, and enjoy.

Wild Alaskan Cod

SERVES
3

MINUTES
8

Nutritional Information Per Serving: 194 calories, 2.2 grams carbohydrates, 20 grams protein, 11 grams fat, 915 mg sodium, 5.3 grams saturated fat.

Ingredients:

1 large fillet of wild Alaskan cod

1 tsp. salt

1 tsp. pepper

3/4 cup sliced cherry tomatoes

2 tbsp. butter

2 tsp. olive oil

1 cup water

Directions:

Using a glass dish that you can put inside your Pressure Cooker, place the cherry tomatoes.

Next, slice the fillet of fish into three pieces, and place the fillet pieces on top of the tomatoes. Add salt and pepper to the top, along with pats of butter. Drizzle the olive oil over the top.

Then, pour the cup of water into the Pressure Cooker, and add the trivet over the top. Place the glass dish over the trivet.

Place the lid on the Pressure Cooker, and lock it. Press the "Manual" button and cook on HIGH pressure for five minutes. If the fish is frozen, cook it for nine minutes instead.

Next, release the pressure immediately, so that the fish doesn't overcook. Serve the fish and tomatoes warm, and enjoy.

WHOLE FOOD
BEEF & PORK PRESSURE COOKER RECIPES

Beef Stroganoff

SERVES
6

MINUTES
30

Nutritional Information Per Serving: 207 calories, 13 grams carbohydrates, 9 grams protein, 13 grams fat, 1049 mg sodium, 7.2 grams saturated fat.

Ingredients:

1 tbsp. olive oil

1 1/2 pounds beef stew, sliced into one-inch cubes

4 minced garlic cloves

1/2 diced onion

12 ounces sliced mushrooms

1/3 cup apple cider vinegar

1 1/2 cup beef broth

1/2 tsp. onion powder

1/2 tsp. garlic powder

1/2 cup coconut milk

1/3 cup coconut aminos

2 tbsp. arrowroot powder mixed with 2 tbsp. water

1 tsp. salt

1 tsp. pepper

Directions:

First, press the "sauté" button on the Pressure Cooker. When it's hot, add the olive oil to the bottom of the Pressure Cooker, and top it with onions. Cook the onions for two minutes. Then, add the garlic, and cook for an additional two minutes. Afterwards, press the "cancel" button.

Next, add onion powder and garlic powder to the beef, along with a bit of salt and pepper. Place the beef on top of the onions.

To the side, stir together the beef broth, apple cider vinegar, and the coconut aminos. Pour this mixture over the top of the meat, and then add the mushrooms.

Next, place the lid on the Pressure Cooker, and secure it. Cook the beef on HIGH for 15 minutes, and then allow the pressure to release naturally (this should take an additional 15 minutes).

Then, remove the lid, and add the coconut milk. Stir well. Add the arrowroot starch, mixed with water, and stir. Allow the mixture to thicken for three minutes.

Serve the beef stroganoff warm, and enjoy.

Chilly Night Beef Stew

SERVES
8

MINUTES
80

Nutritional Information Per Serving: 637 calories, 6 grams carbohydrates, 41 grams protein, 49 grams fat, 532 mg sodium, 26 grams saturated fat.

Ingredients:

5 minced garlic cloves

1 red pepper, without the seeds or stem, chopped into small pieces

2 tbsp. curry powder

4 chopped shallots

1/4 cup beef broth

1/2 tsp. nutmeg

1 tbsp. fish sauce

1 1/2-inch piece of ginger, chopped

8 cashews, chopped coarsely

Meat Ingredients:

2 1/2 pounds boneless chuck roast, chopped into one-inch pieces

2 tbsp. ghee

2 bay leaves

14 ounces coconut milk

1 red pepper, without the seeds and stems, chopped

2 cups spinach

1 cinnamon stick

1 tsp. sea salt

1 tsp. pepper

Directions:

First, stir together the minced garlic cloves, red pepper, curry powder, shallots, beef broth, nutmeg, fish sauce, ginger, and the cashews, and pour the mixture in a blender or a food processor. Blend the mixture until it's smooth. Then, set the mixture to the side.

Next, salt and pepper the beef on all sides in preparation for the next step.

Add the ghee to the Pressure Cooker, and heat on the "sauté" function. Once it's heated, brown the beef in the Pressure Cooker. Once it's browned, set each piece to the side.

Next, pour the mixture from the first step into the Pressure Cooker, and heat on the "sauté" function. Add the bay leaf, cinnamon stick, and coconut milk, and stir well. After cooking for about four minutes, add the beef once more.

Place the Pressure Cooker lid on top and secure it. Press the button that says "Meat/Stew," and set the timer for 40 minutes.

After the Pressure Cooker beeps, allow the Pressure Cooker to release pressure naturally for 15 minutes. Then, remove the rest of the pressure manually. Give the mixture a stir, and remove the bay leaves and the cinnamon stick.

Next, add the red pepper, spinach, salt, and pepper. Stir well, and serve the beef stew warm.

Garlic and Chipotle Beef Barbacoa

SERVES
12

MINUTES
120

Nutritional Information Per Serving: 398 calories, 4 grams carbohydrates, 27 grams protein, 29 grams fat, 339 mg sodium, 11.5 grams saturated fat.

Ingredients:

2 3/4 pounds beef chuck roast, chopped into chunks

7 minced garlic cloves

1 diced onion

1 tsp. pepper

1 tsp. salt

8 ounces green chilies, canned

3 diced chipotle peppers

4 tbsp. coconut vinegar

Juice from 4 limes

1 tbsp. oregano

1/2 cup water

1 tbsp. cumin

Directions:

First, add the entire list of ingredients to the Pressure Cooker, and give the mixture a big stir.

Next, place the lid on the Pressure Cooker, and close the vent. Hit the button that says "Manual," and use the plus button to increase the time to 60 minutes.

After the Pressure Cooker beeps, allow the pressure to release naturally. When it has, remove the lid, and shred the beef with two forks.

At this time, press the "sauté" button. Stir occasionally, allowing the sauce around the beef to reduce. This should take about 40 minutes.

Serve warm, and enjoy.

Caribbean Pork Roast

SERVES
12

MINUTES
60

Nutritional Information Per Serving: 424 calories, 0 grams carbohydrates, 33 grams protein, 31 grams fat, 96 mg sodium, 11.3 grams saturated fat.

Ingredients:

3 3/4 pounds pork shoulder

1 tbsp. olive oil

1/3 cup Badia Jamaican Jerk spice blend

3/4 cup broth or beef stock

Directions:

First, rub the entire pork shoulder with olive oil. Then, coat the pork with the spice blend.

Press the button that says "sauté" on the Pressure Cooker, and make sure to brown the meat on all sides. This should take about three to four minutes on each side.

Next, add the beef broth to the Pressure Cooker, and place the lid on the Pressure Cooker. Seal it. Press the button that says "Manual," and cook on HIGH pressure for 45 minutes.

Afterwards, allow the pressure to release slowly on its own. This should take about 15 minutes.

Then, remove the lid on the Pressure Cooker, making sure to release the steam away from your face.

Shred the pork shoulder using two large forks, and serve warm.

Mexican Pork Carnitas

SERVES
6

MINUTES
120

Nutritional Information Per Serving: 219 calories, 9 grams carbohydrates, 30 grams protein, 6 grams fat, 458 mg sodium, 3.4 grams saturated fat.

Ingredients:

1 1/2 pounds pork, without the bone, sliced into chunks

1/2 tbsp. chili powder

2 tsp. garlic powder

2 tsp. onion powder

1 tsp. black pepper

1 tsp. salt

2 oranges, juiced

1 lime, juiced

1 tbsp. coconut oil

Directions:

First, stir together the spices, and coat them onto the pork—making sure to rub it into the skin.

Next, add the pork to the Pressure Cooker.

To the side, stir together the lime juice and the orange juice in a mixing cup. Add more water, so that the line reaches the "one cup" level. Pour this mixture into the Pressure Cooker at this time.

Next, add the lid to the Pressure Cooker, and seal the valve. Press the "manual" button, and use the "plus" button to mark the timer to 50 minutes.

When the Pressure Cooker beeps, press the button that says "Cancel," and allow the pressure to release from the Pressure Cooker naturally.

Afterwards (about 15 minutes later), remove the lid, and press the button that says "sauté." At this time, use two forks or two tongs to shred the meat in the pot. Allow the liquid at the bottom of the Pressure Cooker to cook away, and stir occasionally, making sure the meat doesn't stick to the bottom.

This process will take about 30 minutes. Afterwards, add the coconut oil, and stir. Cook for about five minutes more, or until the pork begins to brown.

At this time, turn off the Pressure Cooker, and serve the pork warm.

Stunning Pressure Cooker Pork Ragu

SERVES
8

MINUTES
120

Nutritional Information Per Serving: 211 calories, 8.9 grams carbohydrates, 4 grams fat, 32 grams protein, 553 mg sodium, 1.4 grams saturated fat.

Ingredients:

2 pounds pork tenderloin

4 minced garlic cloves

1 tsp. olive oil

1 tsp. salt

1 tsp. black pepper

8 ounces of roasted red peppers from a jar

29 ounces crushed tomatoes

2 bay leaves

1 sprig of fresh thyme

1 1/2 tbsp. chopped parsley

Directions:

First, salt and pepper the pork on all sides.

Next, press the button that says "sauté" on the Pressure Cooker, and add the garlic and the olive oil to the Pressure Cooker. Allow the garlic to sauté for two minutes. Afterwards, remove the garlic with a slotted spoon.

Next, add the pork to the olive oil and brown it for about three minutes on each side.

Next, add the red peppers, crushed tomatoes, bay leaves, thyme, and half of the parsley and give the mixture a stir.

Place the lid on the Pressure Cooker and cook on HIGH pressure for 45 minutes. Afterwards, allow the pressure to release naturally. This should take about 15 minutes.

When 15 minutes is up, remove the lid carefully. Discard the bay leaves, and shred the pork using two forks. Top the pork with what's leftover of the parsley, and serve the warm Ragu over zucchini noodles.

Pulled Pork with Whole Food BBQ Sauce

SERVES
10

MINUTES
120

Nutritional Information Per Serving: 497 calories, 7.4 grams carbohydrates, 31 grams protein, 37 grams fat, 833 mg sodium, 12 grams saturated fat.

Ingredients:

4 pounds of pork shoulder with the bone inside

1 tbsp. smoked paprika

1 tbsp. pepper

1 tbsp. salt

1 tbsp. onion powder

2 cups bone broth

1 tbsp. garlic powder

BBQ Sauce Ingredients:

1/2 cup coconut aminos

5 dates, soaked in water for about an hour prior to using

1/3 cup tomato paste

2 tsp. chili powder

2 tsp. garlic powder

Directions:

First, bring together the pepper, salt, paprika, onion powder, and the garlic powder in a medium-sized bowl. Mix it together well.

Then, slice the pork shoulder into two pieces. Massage each of the pork shoulder pieces with the spices rub.

Then, place the pork in the Pressure Cooker, with the skin up. Place the lid on the Pressure Cooker, and cook on HIGH pressure for 90 minutes, making sure that the vent is closed.

As the pork is cooking in the Pressure Cooker, stir together the BBQ sauce by placing all of the ingredients—from the coconut aminos to the garlic powder, in a blender or a food processor. Process the ingredients well, until they're smooth.

Store the BBQ sauce in the refrigerator until the pork is ready to come out of the Pressure Cooker.

Once the Pressure Cooker beeps, allow the pressure to release naturally. This should take about 15 minutes.

Then, remove the pork from the Pressure Cooker. Place it on a cutting board, and use two tongs or two forks to shred the meat up. Pour the sauce over the meat, stir, and serve.

WHOLE FOOD
SNACK PRESSURE COOKER RECIPES

Spiced Cauliflower Dip

SERVES
4

MINUTES
12

Nutritional Information Per Serving: 150 calories, 16 grams carbohydrates, 8 grams fat, 5 grams protein, 654 mg sodium, 1.6 grams saturated fat.

Ingredients:

4 cups chopped cauliflower florets (probably from one head of cauliflower)

1/2 cup cashews, raw

3 carrots, chopped

2 cups water

1/2 tsp. chili powder

1/2 tsp. paprika

Juice from 20 ounces of diced tomatoes and green chilies

An optional amount of vegetables from diced tomato and green chili cans

1/3 cup chopped red onions

1/2 cup chopped cilantro

1 tsp. salt

1/2 tsp. mustard powder

Directions:

First, add the water, cauliflower, cashews, and the carrots to the Pressure Cooker. Place the lid on the Pressure Cooker and cook on HIGH pressure for six minutes. Afterwards, release the pressure manually, making sure to release the steam away from your face.

Next, pour the mixture over a strainer, draining the water into the sink.

Place the mixture into the blender, along with the spices, the liquid from the can of tomato, and any salt and pepper to taste. Blend the mixture well.

Next, pour out the ingredients from the blender, and add any green chilies and tomatoes from the can, along with the red onions. Add any salt and pepper to taste. Serve the mixture warm or cold, and enjoy.

Middle Eastern Baba Ghanoush

SERVES
4

MINUTES
15

Nutritional Information Per Serving: 171 calories, 11 grams carbohydrates, 14 grams fat, 2.9 grams protein, 302 mg sodium, 2 grams saturated fat.

Ingredients:

1 large-sized eggplant

1 cup water

2 tsp. lemon juice

2 minced garlic cloves

1/2 diced onion

1/2 tsp. cumin

1/2 tsp. salt

2 tbsp. olive oil

1 tbsp. Sesame oil

1/2 tsp. pepper

3 tbsp. toasted sesame seeds

1/2 cup chopped parsley

1/2 tsp. cumin

Directions:

First, put your knife into the eggplant and slice a few inserts into it. Place the eggplant on a trivet in the pressure cooker.

Next, add the one cup of water. Place the lid on the Pressure Cooker, and cook the eggplant on HIGH for eight minutes. After eight minutes, release the pressure immediately, making sure to release the steam away from your face.

Next, remove the eggplant from the Pressure Cooker, and dump the water out of the Pressure Cooker. Peel the eggplant and slice it into smaller pieces.

Press the button that says "sauté" on the Pressure Cooker, and add the sesame seeds and the two types of oil. Toast the seeds for two minutes, and then add the onions and the eggplant.

Cook the eggplant and the onions until they begin to caramelize. This should take about four minutes. Then, add the rest of the ingredients. Stir well to combine.

After three more minutes of cooking, pour the mixture into a blender, or use an immersion blender to blend the mixture to your desired consistency.

Top the baba ghanoush with cumin and parsley, and serve warm.

Healthy BBQ Meatballs

SERVES
4

MINUTES
20

Nutritional Information Per Serving: 293 calories, 18 grams carbohydrates, 9 grams fat, 33 grams protein, 781 mg sodium, 3 grams saturated fat.

Meat Ingredients:

1 pound ground pork

1 egg

1/3 cup chopped onion, sweet

Sauce Ingredients:

1 tbsp. ghee

1/3 cup apple cider vinegar

2 1/2 cups cherries

1 1/2 cups diced onions

1/2 tsp. salt

1/2 tsp. black pepper

3 minced garlic cloves

1 1/4 cup tomato sauce, organic

2 tsp. mustard powder

Directions:

First, turn on the Pressure Cooker and press the "sauté" button. Add the ghee to the Pressure Cooker at this time.

The moment the ghee melts, add 1 1/2 cups onions, and sauté them in the ghee for four minutes. Then, add the garlic, and stir the mixture until it begins to smell. This should take about two minutes.

Next, add the apple cider vinegar, cherries, salt, pepper, tomato sauce, and the mustard powder. Stir well, add the lid on the Pressure Cooker, and then press the button that says MANUAL. Cook the sauce for five minutes.

As the mixture cooks, stir together the pork, sweet onion, and egg, using your hands to make sure you don't overwork the meat. Create meatballs (around 17 or so) with your hands, rolling them into tight balls.

Place the meatballs on a cookie sheet, and add the cookie sheet to the refrigerator.

After the BBQ sauce is completed, release the pressure manually—making sure to release the steam away from your face. Afterwards, remove the lid from the Pressure Cooker.

Add the meat to the Pressure Cooker, and spoon the BBQ mixture over the meatballs, making sure to coat them. Place the lid back to the Pressure Cooker, press the MANUAL button, and cook for 5 minutes.

After five minutes, release the pressure manually, and remove the meatballs using a slotted spoon. Add them to a serving dish.

Next, press the button that says "sauté" once more, and cook the sauce, uncovered, for ten minutes, stirring every few minutes. This will allow the sauce to reduce and become sweet and vibrant for the meatballs.

Serve the meatballs warm, with the sauce over the top.

Soul-Warming Applesauce

SERVES
10

MINUTES
20

Nutritional Information Per Serving: 129 calories, 34 grams carbohydrates, 1 gram protein, .5 gram fat, 235 mg sodium, 0 grams saturated fat.

Ingredients:

11 apples, medium-sized, diced, cored, and peeled

1/2 cup water

2 tsp. cinnamon

1 tsp. salt

Directions:

First, prep the apples and add them to the Pressure Cooker. Add the cinnamon and the salt, and pour the water over the top.

Next, slice a piece of parchment paper so that you have a piece large enough to sit over the top of the apples in the Pressure Cooker.

After you've positioned your parchment paper, place the lid on the Pressure Cooker, and seal the valve. Press the Manual button, and set the timer for 10 minutes.

After the timer beeps, allow the pressure to release from the Pressure Cooker naturally. Afterwards, remove the lid, and remove the parchment paper.

Using a hand blender, blend the mixture well, and then add more cinnamon to taste. Serve either warm or cold, and enjoy.

WHOLE FOOD
SIDE DISH PRESSURE COOKER RECIPES

Super-Fast Brussels Sprouts

SERVES
4

MINUTES
6

Nutritional Information Per Serving: 97 calories, 8 grams carbohydrates, 3 grams protein, 6 grams fat, 4.4 grams saturated fat, 299 mg sodium.

Ingredients:

1 pound Brussels sprouts

3/4 cup yellow onion, sliced

2 tbsp. coconut oil

2 tsp. minced garlic

1/2 cup water

1/2 tsp. salt

1/2 tsp. pepper

3 strips chopped turkey bacon

Directions:

First, press the button on the Pressure Cooker that says "sauté." Next, add the coconut oil to the Pressure Cooker, along with the onion and the garlic. Sauté the ingredients for three minutes, stirring occasionally.

Then, add the chopped bacon to the mixture. Sauté for an additional minute, prior to adding the Brussels sprouts.

Add salt and pepper to taste, and give the mixture a good stir. Place the lid on the Pressure Cooker at this time, and close the vent.

Set the Pressure Cooker on MANUAL and cook for three minutes on LOW pressure.

After three minutes, release the pressure immediately, making sure to release the steam away from your face. Stir the Brussels sprouts well, and remove the liquid. Plate the Brussels sprouts and serve warm.

Simple Nutritional Asparagus

SERVES
4

MINUTES
6

Nutritional Information Per Serving: 23 calories, 4 grams carbohydrates, 2.5 grams protein, 0 grams fat, 2 mg sodium, 0 grams saturated fat.

Ingredients:

1 pound of asparagus, fresh and rinsed, with the edges sliced off

1 cup of water

Directions:

First, place the asparagus on a steamer rack. Place the insert into your Pressure Cooker, and then pour the water over the top.

Place the lid on the Pressure Cooker at this time, and seal the vent. Plug in the Pressure Cooker, and press the button that says "steam." Press the plus and minus buttons to adjust the timer to two minutes.

Next, when the beeper goes off, press the CANCEL button and release the steam immediately.

Remove the steamer basket from the Pressure Cooker at this time. Place the asparagus in a serving bowl, and season the asparagus with salt and pepper.

Serve warm, and enjoy.

Vibrant Butternut Squash

SERVES
6

MINUTES
14

Nutritional Information Per Serving: 68 calories, 17 grams carbohydrates, 1.5 grams protein, 0 grams fat, 7 mg sodium, 0 grams saturated fat.

Ingredients:

2 pounds of butternut squash

1 cup of water

Salt and pepper to taste

Directions:

First, add the steamer basket to the Pressure Cooker, and pour over the water. Slice the squash in half long-ways, and add the two halves to the Pressure Cooker steamer.

Place the lid on the Pressure Cooker, and lock it into place. Press the MANUAL mode and cook the squash on HIGH pressure for 12 minutes.

Afterwards, allow the Pressure Cooker to release its pressure for about five minutes prior to pressing cancel and releasing the pressure manually—making sure to release the steam away from your face.

Remove the pieces of squash to a side mixing bowl, and remove the skin carefully, using a paring knife or just your hands.

Next, mash your squash with a fork, spoon, or a mixer, and add salt and pepper to serve. Enjoy warm.

54045333R00061

Made in the USA
Columbia, SC
25 March 2019